GARDEN PLANNER & LOGBOOK

This Book Belongs To:

....

....

....

Weekly Garden Tasks

Monday	Tuesday	Wednesday	Thursday

Friday	Saturday	Sunday	Comment

Notes

Weekly Garden Tasks

Monday	Tuesday	Wednesday	Thursday

Friday	Saturday	Sunday	Comment

Notes
_____
_____
_____
_____

Weekly Garden Tasks

Monday	Tuesday	Wednesday	Thursday

Friday	Saturday	Sunday	Comment

Notes

Weekly Garden Tasks

Monday	Tuesday	Wednesday	Thursday

Friday	Saturday	Sunday	Comment

Notes
_____
_____
_____

Weekly Garden Tasks

Monday	Tuesday	Wednesday	Thursday

Friday	Saturday	Sunday	Comment

Notes

Weekly Garden Tasks

Monday	Tuesday	Wednesday	Thursday

Friday	Saturday	Sunday	Comment

Notes

Weekly Garden Tasks

Monday	Tuesday	Wednesday	Thursday

Friday	Saturday	Sunday	Comment

Notes

Weekly Garden Tasks

Monday	Tuesday	Wednesday	Thursday

Friday	Saturday	Sunday	Comment

Notes

Weekly Garden Tasks

Monday	Tuesday	Wednesday	Thursday

Friday	Saturday	Sunday	Comment

Notes

Weekly Garden Tasks

Monday	Tuesday	Wednesday	Thursday

Friday	Saturday	Sunday	Comment

Notes

Weekly Garden Tasks

Monday	Tuesday	Wednesday	Thursday

Friday	Saturday	Sunday	Comment

Notes

Weekly Garden Tasks

Monday	Tuesday	Wednesday	Thursday

Friday	Saturday	Sunday	Comment

Notes
_____
_____
_____
_____

Weekly Garden Tasks

Monday	Tuesday	Wednesday	Thursday

Friday	Saturday	Sunday	Comment

Notes

Weekly Garden Tasks

Monday	Tuesday	Wednesday	Thursday

Friday	Saturday	Sunday	Comment

Notes

Weekly Garden Tasks

Monday	Tuesday	Wednesday	Thursday

Friday	Saturday	Sunday	Comment

Notes

Weekly Garden Tasks

Monday	Tuesday	Wednesday	Thursday

Friday	Saturday	Sunday	Comment

Notes

Weekly Garden Tasks

Monday	Tuesday	Wednesday	Thursday

Friday	Saturday	Sunday	Comment

Notes

Weekly Garden Tasks

Monday	Tuesday	Wednesday	Thursday

Friday	Saturday	Sunday	Comment

Notes
_____
_____
_____

Weekly Garden Tasks

Monday	Tuesday	Wednesday	Thursday

Friday	Saturday	Sunday	Comment

Notes

_____

_____

_____

Weekly Garden Tasks

Monday	Tuesday	Wednesday	Thursday
Friday	Saturday	Sunday	Comment

Notes
_____
_____
_____

Weekly Garden Tasks

Monday	Tuesday	Wednesday	Thursday

Friday	Saturday	Sunday	Comment

Notes

Weekly Garden Tasks

Monday	Tuesday	Wednesday	Thursday

Friday	Saturday	Sunday	Comment

Notes

Weekly Garden Tasks

Monday	Tuesday	Wednesday	Thursday

Friday	Saturday	Sunday	Comment

Notes

Weekly Garden Tasks

Monday	Tuesday	Wednesday	Thursday

Friday	Saturday	Sunday	Comment

Notes

Weekly Garden Tasks

Monday	Tuesday	Wednesday	Thursday
Friday	Saturday	Sunday	Comment

Notes

Weekly Garden Tasks

Monday	Tuesday	Wednesday	Thursday

Friday	Saturday	Sunday	Comment

Notes
_____
_____
_____

Weekly Garden Tasks

Monday	Tuesday	Wednesday	Thursday

Friday	Saturday	Sunday	Comment

Notes

Weekly Garden Tasks

Monday	Tuesday	Wednesday	Thursday

Friday	Saturday	Sunday	Comment

Notes
_____
_____
_____

Weekly Garden Tasks

Monday	Tuesday	Wednesday	Thursday

Friday	Saturday	Sunday	Comment

Notes

Weekly Garden Tasks

Monday	Tuesday	Wednesday	Thursday

Friday	Saturday	Sunday	Comment

Notes

Weekly Garden Tasks

Monday	Tuesday	Wednesday	Thursday

Friday	Saturday	Sunday	Comment

Notes

Weekly Garden Tasks

Monday	Tuesday	Wednesday	Thursday

Friday	Saturday	Sunday	Comment

Notes
_____
_____
_____

Weekly Garden Tasks

Monday	Tuesday	Wednesday	Thursday

Friday	Saturday	Sunday	Comment

Notes

Weekly Garden Tasks

Monday	Tuesday	Wednesday	Thursday

Friday	Saturday	Sunday	Comment

Notes
_____
_____
_____
_____

Weekly Garden Tasks

Monday	Tuesday	Wednesday	Thursday

Friday	Saturday	Sunday	Comment

Notes

Weekly Garden Tasks

Monday	Tuesday	Wednesday	Thursday

Friday	Saturday	Sunday	Comment

Notes

Weekly Garden Tasks

Monday	Tuesday	Wednesday	Thursday

Friday	Saturday	Sunday	Comment

Notes

Weekly Garden Tasks

Monday	Tuesday	Wednesday	Thursday

Friday	Saturday	Sunday	Comment

Notes

Weekly Garden Tasks

Monday	Tuesday	Wednesday	Thursday

Friday	Saturday	Sunday	Comment

Notes

Weekly Garden Tasks

Monday	Tuesday	Wednesday	Thursday

Friday	Saturday	Sunday	Comment

Notes
_____
_____
_____

Weekly Garden Tasks

Monday	Tuesday	Wednesday	Thursday

Friday	Saturday	Sunday	Comment

Notes

Weekly Garden Tasks

Monday	Tuesday	Wednesday	Thursday

Friday	Saturday	Sunday	Comment

Notes
_____
_____
_____
_____

Weekly Garden Tasks

Monday	Tuesday	Wednesday	Thursday

Friday	Saturday	Sunday	Comment

Notes

Weekly Garden Tasks

Monday	Tuesday	Wednesday	Thursday

Friday	Saturday	Sunday	Comment

Notes
_____
_____
_____
_____

Weekly Garden Tasks

Monday	Tuesday	Wednesday	Thursday

Friday	Saturday	Sunday	Comment

Notes

Weekly Garden Tasks

Monday	Tuesday	Wednesday	Thursday

Friday	Saturday	Sunday	Comment

Notes

Weekly Garden Tasks

Monday	Tuesday	Wednesday	Thursday

Friday	Saturday	Sunday	Comment

Notes

Weekly Garden Tasks

Monday	Tuesday	Wednesday	Thursday

Friday	Saturday	Sunday	Comment

Notes

Weekly Garden Tasks

Monday	Tuesday	Wednesday	Thursday

Friday	Saturday	Sunday	Comment

Notes

Weekly Garden Tasks

Monday	Tuesday	Wednesday	Thursday

Friday	Saturday	Sunday	Comment

Notes

Weekly Garden Tasks

Monday	Tuesday	Wednesday	Thursday

Friday	Saturday	Sunday	Comment

Notes

Weekly Garden Tasks

Monday	Tuesday	Wednesday	Thursday

Friday	Saturday	Sunday	Comment

Notes

Shopping List

Product/Amount	Price	Product/Amount	Price

Shopping List

Product/Amount	Price	Product/Amount	Price

Shopping List

Product/Amount	Price	Product/Amount	Price

Shopping List

Product/Amount	Price	Product/Amount	Price

Shopping List

Product/Amount	Price	Product/Amount	Price

Shopping List

Product/Amount	Price	Product/Amount	Price

Shopping List

Product/Amount	Price	Product/Amount	Price

Shopping List

Product/Amount	Price	Product/Amount	Price

Seed Starting Log

Plant Name	Variety
Seed Source	Date Planted
Germination Date	Location

Plant Name	Variety
Seed Source	Date Planted
Germination Date	Location

Plant Name	Variety
Seed Source	Date Planted
Germination Date	Location

Seed Starting Log

Plant Name	Variety
Seed Source	Date Planted
Germination Date	Location

Plant Name	Variety
Seed Source	Date Planted
Germination Date	Location

Plant Name	Variety
Seed Source	Date Planted
Germination Date	Location

Seed Starting Log

Plant Name	Variety
Seed Source	Date Planted
Germination Date	Location

Plant Name	Variety
Seed Source	Date Planted
Germination Date	Location

Plant Name	Variety
Seed Source	Date Planted
Germination Date	Location

Seed Starting Log

Plant Name	Variety
Seed Source	Date Planted
Germination Date	Location

Plant Name	Variety
Seed Source	Date Planted
Germination Date	Location

Plant Name	Variety
Seed Source	Date Planted
Germination Date	Location

Seed Starting Log

Plant Name	Variety
Seed Source	Date Planted
Germination Date	Location

Plant Name	Variety
Seed Source	Date Planted
Germination Date	Location

Plant Name	Variety
Seed Source	Date Planted
Germination Date	Location

Seed Starting Log

Plant Name	Variety
Seed Source	Date Planted
Germination Date	Location

Plant Name	Variety
Seed Source	Date Planted
Germination Date	Location

Plant Name	Variety
Seed Source	Date Planted
Germination Date	Location

Seed Starting Log

Plant Name	Variety
Seed Source	Date Planted
Germination Date	Location

Plant Name	Variety
Seed Source	Date Planted
Germination Date	Location

Plant Name	Variety
Seed Source	Date Planted
Germination Date	Location

Seed Starting Log

Plant Name	Variety
Seed Source	Date Planted
Germination Date	Location

Plant Name	Variety
Seed Source	Date Planted
Germination Date	Location

Plant Name	Variety
Seed Source	Date Planted
Germination Date	Location

Seed Starting Log

Plant Name	Variety
Seed Source	Date Planted
Germination Date	Location

Plant Name	Variety
Seed Source	Date Planted
Germination Date	Location

Plant Name	Variety
Seed Source	Date Planted
Germination Date	Location

Seed Starting Log

Plant Name	Variety
Seed Source	Date Planted
Germination Date	Location

Plant Name	Variety
Seed Source	Date Planted
Germination Date	Location

Plant Name	Variety
Seed Source	Date Planted
Germination Date	Location

Seed Starting Log

Plant Name	Variety
Seed Source	Date Planted
Germination Date	Location

Plant Name	Variety
Seed Source	Date Planted
Germination Date	Location

Plant Name	Variety
Seed Source	Date Planted
Germination Date	Location

Seed Starting Log

Plant Name	Variety
Seed Source	Date Planted
Germination Date	Location

Plant Name	Variety
Seed Source	Date Planted
Germination Date	Location

Plant Name	Variety
Seed Source	Date Planted
Germination Date	Location

Seed Starting Log

Plant Name	Variety
Seed Source	Date Planted
Germination Date	Location

Plant Name	Variety
Seed Source	Date Planted
Germination Date	Location

Plant Name	Variety
Seed Source	Date Planted
Germination Date	Location

Seed Starting Log

Plant Name	Variety
Seed Source	Date Planted
Germination Date	Location

Plant Name	Variety
Seed Source	Date Planted
Germination Date	Location

Plant Name	Variety
Seed Source	Date Planted
Germination Date	Location

Seed Starting Log

Plant Name	Variety
Seed Source	Date Planted
Germination Date	Location

Plant Name	Variety
Seed Source	Date Planted
Germination Date	Location

Plant Name	Variety
Seed Source	Date Planted
Germination Date	Location

Seed Starting Log

Plant Name	Variety
Seed Source	Date Planted
Germination Date	Location

Plant Name	Variety
Seed Source	Date Planted
Germination Date	Location

Plant Name	Variety
Seed Source	Date Planted
Germination Date	Location

Seed Starting Log

Plant Name	Variety
Seed Source	Date Planted
Germination Date	Location

Plant Name	Variety
Seed Source	Date Planted
Germination Date	Location

Plant Name	Variety
Seed Source	Date Planted
Germination Date	Location

Seed Starting Log

Plant Name	Variety
Seed Source	Date Planted
Germination Date	Location

Plant Name	Variety
Seed Source	Date Planted
Germination Date	Location

Plant Name	Variety
Seed Source	Date Planted
Germination Date	Location

Pests and Problem

Problem			Problem	
Plants			Plants	
Date Applied			Date Applied	
Treatment			Treatment	
Notes			Notes	
Problem			Problem	
Plants			Plants	
Date Applied			Date Applied	
Treatment			Treatment	
Notes			Notes	
Problem			Problem	
Plants			Plants	
Date Applied			Date Applied	
Treatment			Treatment	
Notes			Notes	

Pests and Problem

Problem			Problem	
Plants			Plants	
Date Applied			Date Applied	
Treatment			Treatment	
Notes			Notes	

Problem			Problem	
Plants			Plants	
Date Applied			Date Applied	
Treatment			Treatment	
Notes			Notes	

Problem			Problem	
Plants			Plants	
Date Applied			Date Applied	
Treatment			Treatment	
Notes			Notes	

Pests and Problem

Problem	
Plants	
Date Applied	
Treatment	
Notes	

Problem	
Plants	
Date Applied	
Treatment	
Notes	

Problem	
Plants	
Date Applied	
Treatment	
Notes	

Problem	
Plants	
Date Applied	
Treatment	
Notes	

Problem	
Plants	
Date Applied	
Treatment	
Notes	

Problem	
Plants	
Date Applied	
Treatment	
Notes	

Pests and Problem

Problem			Problem	
Plants			Plants	
Date Applied			Date Applied	
Treatment			Treatment	
Notes			Notes	

Problem			Problem	
Plants			Plants	
Date Applied			Date Applied	
Treatment			Treatment	
Notes			Notes	

Problem			Problem	
Plants			Plants	
Date Applied			Date Applied	
Treatment			Treatment	
Notes			Notes	

Pests and Problem

Problem			Problem	
Plants			Plants	
Date Applied			Date Applied	
Treatment			Treatment	
Notes			Notes	

Problem			Problem	
Plants			Plants	
Date Applied			Date Applied	
Treatment			Treatment	
Notes			Notes	

Problem			Problem	
Plants			Plants	
Date Applied			Date Applied	
Treatment			Treatment	
Notes			Notes	

Pests and Problem

Problem			Problem	
Plants			Plants	
Date Applied			Date Applied	
Treatment			Treatment	
Notes			Notes	
Problem			Problem	
Plants			Plants	
Date Applied			Date Applied	
Treatment			Treatment	
Notes			Notes	
Problem			Problem	
Plants			Plants	
Date Applied			Date Applied	
Treatment			Treatment	
Notes			Notes	

Pests and Problem

Problem	
Plants	
Date Applied	
Treatment	
Notes	

Problem	
Plants	
Date Applied	
Treatment	
Notes	

Problem	
Plants	
Date Applied	
Treatment	
Notes	

Problem	
Plants	
Date Applied	
Treatment	
Notes	

Problem	
Plants	
Date Applied	
Treatment	
Notes	

Problem	
Plants	
Date Applied	
Treatment	
Notes	

Pests and Problem

Problem			Problem	
Plants			Plants	
Date Applied			Date Applied	
Treatment			Treatment	
Notes			Notes	

Problem			Problem	
Plants			Plants	
Date Applied			Date Applied	
Treatment			Treatment	
Notes			Notes	

Problem			Problem	
Plants			Plants	
Date Applied			Date Applied	
Treatment			Treatment	
Notes			Notes	

Pests and Problem

Problem			Problem	
Plants			Plants	
Date Applied			Date Applied	
Treatment			Treatment	
Notes			Notes	

Problem			Problem	
Plants			Plants	
Date Applied			Date Applied	
Treatment			Treatment	
Notes			Notes	

Problem			Problem	
Plants			Plants	
Date Applied			Date Applied	
Treatment			Treatment	
Notes			Notes	

Pests and Problem

Problem			Problem	
Plants			Plants	
Date Applied			Date Applied	
Treatment			Treatment	
Notes			Notes	

Problem			Problem	
Plants			Plants	
Date Applied			Date Applied	
Treatment			Treatment	
Notes			Notes	

Problem			Problem	
Plants			Plants	
Date Applied			Date Applied	
Treatment			Treatment	
Notes			Notes	

Pests and Problem

Problem			Problem	
Plants			Plants	
Date Applied			Date Applied	
Treatment			Treatment	
Notes			Notes	

Problem			Problem	
Plants			Plants	
Date Applied			Date Applied	
Treatment			Treatment	
Notes			Notes	

Problem			Problem	
Plants			Plants	
Date Applied			Date Applied	
Treatment			Treatment	
Notes			Notes	

Pests and Problem

Problem			Problem	
Plants			Plants	
Date Applied			Date Applied	
Treatment			Treatment	
Notes			Notes	
Problem			Problem	
Plants			Plants	
Date Applied			Date Applied	
Treatment			Treatment	
Notes			Notes	
Problem			Problem	
Plants			Plants	
Date Applied			Date Applied	
Treatment			Treatment	
Notes			Notes	

Harvest Tracker

Plant	Date Planted	Day to Harvest	Quantity

Harvest Tracker

Plant	Date Planted	Day to Harvest	Quantity

Harvest Tracker

Plant	Date Planted	Day to Harvest	Quantity

Harvest Tracker

Plant	Date Planted	Day to Harvest	Quantity

Harvest Tracker

Plant	Date Planted	Day to Harvest	Quantity

Harvest Tracker

Plant	Date Planted	Day to Harvest	Quantity

Harvest Tracker

Plant	Date Planted	Day to Harvest	Quantity

Harvest Tracker

Plant	Date Planted	Day to Harvest	Quantity

Harvest Tracker

Plant	Date Planted	Day to Harvest	Quantity

Harvest Tracker

Plant	Date Planted	Day to Harvest	Quantity

Harvest Tracker

Plant	Date Planted	Day to Harvest	Quantity

Harvest Tracker

Plant	Date Planted	Day to Harvest	Quantity

Harvest Tracker

Plant	Date Planted	Day to Harvest	Quantity

Harvest Tracker

Plant	Date Planted	Day to Harvest	Quantity

Garden Journaling

Garden Journaling

Garden Journaling

Garden Journaling

Garden Journaling

Garden Journaling

Garden Journaling

Garden Journaling

Garden Journaling

Garden Journaling

Garden Journaling

Garden Journaling

Garden Journaling

Garden Journaling

Garden Journaling

Made in the USA
Las Vegas, NV
08 March 2021